LIFE IN THE PAST

ANCIENT ROME

Jane Bingham

Adapted from an original text by Richard Dargie

FRANKLIN WATTS
LONDON·SYDNEY

First published in 2009 by Franklin Watts

Copyright © 2009 Arcturus Publishing Limited

Franklin Watts
338 Euston Road
London NW1 3BH

Franklin Watts Australia
Level 17/207 Kent Street, Sydney, NSW 2000

Produced by Arcturus Publishing Limited,
26/27 Bickels Yard, 151–153 Bermondsey Street, London SE1 3HA

Life in the Past is based on the series *Rich and Poor*, published by Franklin Watts.

Editor: Alex Woolf
Designer: Tim Mayer and Mike Reynolds
Illustrator: Adam Hook
Picture researcher: Glass Onion Pictures

Picture Credits
Art Archive: 4 (Rheinischeslandesmuseum Bonn / Dagli Orti), 6 (Dagli Orti), 7 (Museo della Civilta Romana, Rome / Dagli Orti), 8 (Dagli Orti), 10 (Egyptian Museum, Cairo / Dagli Orti), 12 (Archaeological Museum, Naples / Dagli Orti), 13 (Archaeological Museum, Naples / Dagli Orti [A]), 14 (Archaeological Museum, Naples / Dagli Orti [A]), 15 (Museo della Civilta Romana, Rome / Dagli Orti), 19 (Museo della Civilta Romana, Rome / Dagli Orti), 20 (Dagli Orti), 21 (Museo Nazionale Terme, Rome / Dagli Orti), 22 (Bardo Museum, Tunis / Dagli Orti), 23 (Museo della Civilta Romana, Rome / Dagli Orti), 25 (National Museum, Bucharest / Dagli Orti), 26 (Dagli Orti), 27 (Archaeological Museum, Naples / Dagli Orti), 28 (Provinciaal Museum G M Kam Nijmegen, Netherlands / Dagli Orti).
Bridgeman Art Library: 16 (Rheinisches Landesmuseum, Trier, Germany).
Shutterstock: cover (Cornel Achirei).

Every attempt has been made to clear copyright. Should there be any inadvertent omission, please apply to the publisher for rectification.

A CIP catalogue record for this book is available from the British Library.

Dewey Decimal Classification Number: 937

ISBN 978 0 7496 9045 8

Printed in China

Franklin Watts is a division of Hachette Children's Books, an Hachette UK Company
www.hachette.co.uk

· CONTENTS ·

Rulers of Rome

For 500 years, Rome was the richest city in the world. It was the capital of a huge empire. Great wealth poured into Rome from the empire. The noble families who ruled Rome became very rich.

Senators and Knights

The richest Roman nobles were the **senators**. They made laws for the Roman people.

The next rank were the **equestrians**, or knights. They helped to govern Rome.

This carving shows a Roman knight with his horse.

Gentlemen Farmers

Many Roman nobles had a farm in the country. The Roman writer Cicero thought all nobles should be farmers:

'Of all the occupations, none is more suitable than owning a farm.'

From the letters of Marcus Tullius Cicero

The Roman Poor

The ordinary Romans were called **plebeians**. Plebeians were poor, but they had some rights. In early Roman times, they could vote for their leaders.

The poorest people in Rome were the slaves. Some slaves were prisoners captured in wars. Some were the children of slaves.

A Slave's Life

Life was hard for many slaves. They often died young, worn out by hard work. Other slaves had an easier life, working in rich people's homes. A few clever slaves had jobs as doctors, teachers or artists.

Slaves in the home looked after their masters. They also did some cleaning work.

Houses for the Rich

This painting shows some large town houses by a river. They belonged to very rich Romans.

Most wealthy Romans lived in a *domus*. This was a large town house built from brick or stone.

The rooms in a *domus* were arranged in a square around a courtyard. Often there was a pool in the courtyard.

Luxury and Comfort

In the summer, the *domus* stayed cool. In winter, underfloor heating kept people warm. There were paintings on the walls and **mosaics** on the floor.

Flats for the Poor

Poorer Romans usually lived in flats. The flats were part of tall buildings called **insulae**. The *insulae* were very badly built. Sometimes they even fell down.

Unhealthy and Dangerous

The *insulae* had no lavatories and no running water. They also had no kitchens. People cooked on wood stoves that often caught fire.

The *insulae* were built very close together. Fire and diseases spread very fast from one building to the next.

Time to Leave

The writer Cicero bought some flats to rent out to tenants, but big cracks spread through the walls:

'My tenants have all left – and so have the mice!'

From the Letters of Marcus Tullius Cicero

Nobles at Home

In rich Roman families, the father was in charge. Even grown-up men had to obey their fathers. Women had very few rights.

Noblemen married a wife from another noble family. When she got married, the wife gave her husband money and land.

This carving shows a group of noble Roman families.

Lessons for the Rich

All rich children learned to read and write. They were taught by slaves called tutors. Older boys learned about law and government. Girls were trained to run a home.

A Loving Wife

The Roman writer Pliny had a young wife who was devoted to him:

'She keeps copies of my works to read again and again.... She has even set my verses to music and sings them, to the accompaniment of her **lyre**.'

From the letters of Pliny the Younger

Plebeian Families

When a poor man wanted to get married, he gave a gift to his new wife's family. Then he took his wife home with him. The groom carried his bride through the door of his house.

Learning a Trade

Most children from poor families did not learn to read or write. Instead, they helped their parents with their work. Children learned a trade by working with their parents.

A Roman craftsman teaches his son how to make a **mosaic**.

Some poor parents had too many children to feed. They abandoned their babies or sold them as slaves.

Fine Fashions

Wealthy Roman men wore a **toga**. This was a sheet of cloth draped around the body. Togas were usually plain white. **Senators'** togas were edged with purple.

Rich Roman women wore a long dress. It was called a *stola*.

Fancy Footwear

The Romans wore shoes that showed their rank. Noblemen wore red sandals. Noblewomen wore white or yellow shoes.

Top Togas

Romans were very proud of their togas. The poet Virgil described the Romans as:

'the Lords of the World, the race that wears the toga'.

From Virgil's *Aeneid* Book I

This statue shows a Roman goddess. She is wearing a *stola* and a shawl.

Clothes for Commoners

Most poor men wore a tunic. Summer tunics were made from linen. Winter tunics were made from wool. Over their tunic, they wore a simple cloak.

Poor Roman women wore a simple dress called a *tunica*. When they went out, women wore a long shawl called a *palla*. The *palla* covered the head and shoulders.

No Trousers!

In later Roman times, some working men began to wear trousers. But Emperor Honorius hated them. He did not allow any trousers in Rome.

Some slaves wore a special uniform. This slave has a uniform with black stripes.

Feasting and Dieting

Some Roman nobles ate far too much. Sometimes they had dinners with more than ten main courses. After each course, the guests had a salty drink. This made them vomit up their food. Then they went on to the next course.

Roman feasts included some very strange dishes. At one dinner, people ate flamingo tongues and camel heels!

Stop Eating!

Many wealthy Romans were overweight. Doctors tried hard to make people diet. Even the government tried to stop the feasts. They banned fancy foods, such as oysters.

This painting shows Romans enjoying a feast. The guests are served by slaves.

Meals for the Masses

Many Romans were too poor to buy food. But they did not starve. Instead, the government gave them bread or wheat. People boiled the wheat to make porridge.

Slaves were given food by their masters. They usually ate bread made from barley. Barley bread was thick, grey and chewy.

Fast Food

Many Romans bought food in the street. Snack bars sold sausages and meat in spicy sauce.

Very poor families were given free bread each morning.

Shopping List

A **plebeian** from Pompeii spent his money as follows:

'*one ass spent on cheese, eight asses on bread, three on oil and three on wine.*' Graffiti from Pompeii

Doctors and Dentists

Rich Romans had toilets and baths at home. This helped them to stay healthy. If they were ill, they called in a doctor.

Tooth Trouble

Wealthy Romans had any rotting teeth pulled out. Then a dentist gave them some false teeth. One dentist sold an ointment to stop tooth decay. It was made of worms and spiders' eggs!

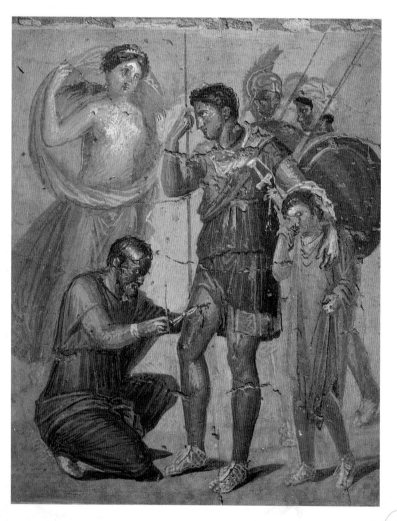

A doctor treats a wounded soldier. Roman doctors could perform simple operations.

Beauty Tip

Not everyone could afford a dentist. The poet Ovid advised poor girls to hide their bad teeth:

'Learn to laugh quietly and cover your teeth with your lips, and you will be thought beautiful.'

From Ovid's *Ars Amatoria*

Danger and Disease

Most poor Romans died before they were 50. Many were worn out by hard work. Some had serious accidents. Others died from breathing poisonous fumes.

Staying Clean

The **River Tiber** in Rome was very dirty. It was full of sewage and rotting food. In the hot summer months, many people died from disease. **Typhoid** and **malaria** were very common.

The government wanted everyone to stay clean and healthy. They encouraged the poor to wash in the public baths. During the summer, entry to the baths was free.

Poor Romans went to a pharmacy when they were sick. The pharmacist sold them ointments and medicines.

Ladies of Leisure

Rich women spent a lot of time getting dressed. They had many slaves to help them.

Roman women had to obey their husbands at all times. They were not allowed to vote or get divorced. If they went to the theatre, wives could not sit with their husbands. They had to sit in seats for women only.

Rich Roman women ran the family home. In the morning, they sent slaves to the market. Later they went to the public baths.

Beauty Care

Wealthy women used many creams on their skin. They also chewed scented sweets to sweeten their breath.

Working Women

Many **plebeian** women had jobs. Some kept inns and shops. Some worked as spinners or weavers of cloth. Wives often helped their husband in his business.

Female slaves worked long hours and had no rights. Even their children belonged to their master.

Using Make-Up

Most Roman women wore make-up. But the plebeian women used very cheap **cosmetics**. Some of them rubbed chalk onto their faces. When it rained the chalk became smeared.

Some poor women trained as gladiators. They had to fight in public shows.

A Good Wife

A Roman wife called Amymone was praised on her tombstone. The inscription said that she was:

'a gifted spinner of wool who built a good home'.

From a tomb inscription in Rome

Nobleman at Work

Roman noblemen saw it as their duty to help the poor. Every morning, people in need went to the nobleman's house. He gave them gifts of money or food.

Noblemen worked as lawyers, bankers and politicians. Lawyers gave advice and supported clients in the law courts. Bankers lent money to traders. Politicians made speeches and passed laws.

Busy Lives

Noblemen also went to many social events. They attended **coming-of-age ceremonies**, engagement parties and weddings.

Roman nobles sent many letters. They dictated their letters to a **scribe**.

Earning a Living

This carving shows a butcher working in his shop.

Many poorer Romans had no job. They depended on gifts from nobles.

Other Romans worked as craftworkers or shopkeepers. Some skilled craftsworkers earned very good money. A tailor could charge 60 **denarii** (about £300) to make a cloak.

Low Wages

Unskilled labourers struggled to earn a living. The men who cleaned the sewers were paid just four denarii (about £20) per day.

Jobs for the Poor

The emperor Vespasian liked to give jobs to the poor. He paid them to build fountains and monuments. Vespasian did not mind if the work took a long time. He said:

'You must allow me to feed my poor common people.'

From *The Life of Vespasian* by Gaius Suetonius Tranquillus

A Grand Day Out

Romans of all classes loved to watch the games. They crowded into large **amphitheatres** to watch violent sports. **Gladiator** fights were especially popular. Wealthy nobles often paid for games and chariot races. They hoped that this would make them popular.

Special Seats

In the amphitheatre, the most important Romans sat in the front row. The emperor had a special balcony. Very rich families had their own marble chairs.

The Colosseum was the biggest amphitheatre in Rome. It could hold 60,000 people.

Fun for All

A group of **plebeians** enjoy a ball game. The government encouraged all Roman citizens to stay fit.

Most poor families went to the games. Entry was free for all, but the poor had to sit near the back. The seats with the worst view were left for women and slaves.

Holidays

The Romans had many public holidays. On these days, people often gathered in large open spaces. They enjoyed wrestling and playing ball games.

Bread and Circuses

The emperors paid huge sums of money for the games. One Roman writer explained why they did it:

'A wise emperor knows that the Roman people are kept loyal by a supply of free grain and by the games.' From the letters of Marcus Cornelius Fronto

Holiday Homes

Some wealthy Romans owned farms in the country. They usually spent the summer on their farm. There they enjoyed the countryside, far away from the busy city.

At the heart of the farm was a cool, comfortable villa. This mosaic shows a villa surrounded by animals and trees.

The Country Life

Some landowners took an interest in farming. Some saw their villa as a peaceful place to get on with their writing. They also enjoyed country sports, such as hunting.

Working on a Farm

In this carving, a goatherd milks one of his flock.

Choosing a Manager

The writer Columella advised farm owners to chose their *vilicus* carefully:

'He should know a lot about farming tasks and also be able to order the other slaves without being too cruel.'

From *On Agriculture* by Lucius Columella

Roman farms were run by an experienced slave called a *vilicus*. He was in charge of a large staff of slaves.

Most farm slaves had a very hard life. Many had chains on their legs to stop them running away.

Costly Slaves

In later Roman times, skilled farm slaves became very expensive. Most landowners hired free men to work on the farm.

Senior Soldiers

Most noblemen spent three years as an army officer. They were put in charge of a large number of men. The most important officer was the *legatus*. He was helped by six officers called **tribunes**.

Glory and Reward

Some Roman nobles stayed in the army for their whole career. They hoped to win many victories. Successful soldiers were rewarded with land and honours.

Victory Parade

The writer Flavius Josephus described the victory parade of the emperor Vespasian:

'All the **legion** marched through Rome in companies and by rank behind their commanders.... The troops shouted with joy and acclaimed Vespasian's bravery.'

From *The Jewish War* by Flavius Josephus

The *legatus* commanded a legion of five or six thousand men.

Life in the Legion

Poorer Roman citizens fought as foot soldiers. They were known as **legionaries**.

Legionaries usually lived in **barracks**. They shared their living space with 20 other men.

Legionaries were paid a wage, but some of this money was used to pay for food, uniform and weapons. If a legionary survived for 25 years, he could retire. He was given a house and some farmland.

Skilful Centurions

The best foot soldiers became **centurions**. They were in charge of 80 to 100 men.

Roman legionaries had to be builders as well as fighters. They built the wooden forts where the soldiers lived.

Solemn Ceremonies

Romans of all classes worshipped the gods. Two of the most important gods were Ceres and Vesta. Ceres was the goddess of the harvest. Vesta looked after the home.

Sacrifices and Signs

Only nobles could be priests. They held ceremonies in temples. Sometimes a priest performed a **sacrifice**. He put an animal to death on a public altar.

Some priests told the future. They studied the weather and the actions of holy birds. Then they explained these signs from the gods.

There were more than 90 temples in Rome. Some of these temples still survive today.

Different Faiths

All the Romans believed in **ancestor** spirits. Even the poorest home had a **shrine** to the ancestors. It was called a *lararium*. Every day the family held prayers at the *lararium*. They also gave presents of food to the spirits.

Christianity Spreads

From 60 CE Christianity spread rapidly. Many poorer Romans became Christians. They prayed that they would have a better life after death.

Many poorer Roman worshipped foreign gods. Here, people worship the goddess Isis from Egypt.

Spring Prayers

Every spring, Roman farmers asked the gods for good weather. The writer Cato described this ceremony:

*'Offer Jupiter a feast of roasted meat and an **urn** of wine, and honour him with prayers. After the offering, plant garlic, millet and lentils in the fields.'*

From *On Agriculture* by Marcus Porcius Cato the Elder

Grieving for the Great

Funerals for nobles were very grand. After a nobleman died, his body was dressed in his finest **toga**. Then it was placed in a chair.

Slaves carried the chair through the city. They were followed by mourners, who sang sad hymns.

Ashes and Tombs

Rich Romans were usually **cremated**. Their ashes were placed inside a stone tomb. The tombs of noblemen stood beside the roads that led into Rome.

After a noble died, a mask of his face was made from wax. Then a death mask was cast in metal.

Budget Burials

When a poor man died, a cypress branch was placed outside the door of his home. Relatives and friends carried the body to the place where it would be cremated.

Funeral Clubs

Some Roman men belonged to a funeral club. They paid a small fee every month. When they died, their ashes were placed in a special house called a *columbarium*.

Most slaves did not have a funeral ceremony. They were buried in a big pit.

Funerals for poor people were often held at night.

Beautiful Memories

Some Roman tomb inscriptions were quite humorous. An inscription for a woman who died in 135 CE includes the words:

'Here is the ugly tomb of a lovely woman called Claudia'.

From a tomb inscription in Rome

BCE

753	The city of Rome is set up, according to legend.
510	Rome becomes a republic. It is ruled by senators.
27	Augustus becomes the first Roman emperor. This is the start of the Roman Empire.

CE

c. 30	Jesus Christ is put to death in Jerusalem.
64	The Great Fire of Rome. Hundreds of Roman *insulae* (flats) are destroyed.
79	The volcano Vesuvius erupts. The town of Pompeii is destroyed.
80	The Colosseum is opened.
c. 100	Over one million people live in the city of Rome.
180	The Roman Empire reaches its greatest size.
212	The emperor Caracalla opens some vast public baths in Rome.
286	The emperor Diocletian splits the Roman Empire into two parts: the Western Empire and the Eastern Empire.
337	The emperor Constantine becomes a Christian.
410	Rome is attacked by tribes of Visigoths.
476	The Western Roman Empire collapses. (The Eastern Roman Empire lasts for another thousand years.)

Books

Colosseum: Rome's Arena of Death
by Peter Connolly (BBC Consumer Publishing, 2003)
Look Inside a Roman Villa
by Richard Dargie (Wayland, 2002)
Picturing the Past: Ancient Rome
by Richard Dargie (Franklin Watts, 2004)
Roman Army
by Ruth Brocklehurst (Usborne Publishing, 2003)
Rome: In Spectacular Cross-Section
by Andrew Solway and Stephen Biesty (Scholastic, 2003)
Virtual History Tours: Look Around a Roman Villa
by Jane Bingham (Franklin Watts, 2007)

CD-Roms, Videos, DVDs and Audiocassettes

Ancient Rome (Castle Home Video, 2001)
Ancient Rome: A Journey Back in Time (Cromwell Video Productions, 2000)
The Romans (Arcventure Interactive CD-Rom, 2002)
The Romans in Europe (Cromwell DVD Productions, 2003)
The Romans in North Africa (Cromwell DVD Productions, 2003)
The Rotten Romans by Terry Deary (BBC Audiobooks, 2003)

Websites

www.bbc.co.uk/history/ancient/romans/
www.historyforkids.org/learn/romans/
www.roman-empire.net/
www.schoolshistory.org.uk/romanpublichealth.htm

amphitheatre A large stadium where public games were held.

ancestor Family members who lived a long time ago.

barracks Large buildings where soldiers live.

centurion An officer in the Roman army. Centurions were in charge of 80 to 100 men.

coming-of-age ceremony A Roman family gathering, held to mark the time when a child became an adult.

cosmetics Make-up.

cremated When a dead body is burned rather than buried.

denarius (plural: denarii) A valuable silver coin used in ancient Rome.

equestrian A Roman knight. Equestrians were members of the noble class.

gladiator A trained fighter who fought one-to-one battles to entertain the public. Gladiators fought in amphitheatres.

insulae Large Roman buildings, divided into flats. *Insulae* were usually three or four storeys high.

legion A very large group of soldiers in the Roman army. A legion was made up of between five and six thousand men.

legionary A Roman soldier who fought on foot.

lyre A stringed instrument shaped like the letter U.

malaria A fever passed on to humans by mosquito bites.

mosaic A pattern or picture made from many small pieces of stone or glass.

pharmacy A shop where people can buy medicines.

plebeian One of the ordinary citizens of Rome.

River Tiber The river that flows through central Italy and Rome to the western Mediterranean.

sacrifice Kill an animal as an offering to a god or goddess.

scribe Someone who was paid to write things down.

senator A noble who was a member of the Roman senate – the main council of government in Rome during the time of the Roman Republic (from c. 509 to 27 BCE).

shrine A holy place where images of the gods were placed.

toga A long robe for men, worn draped around the body. Only Roman citizens had the right to wear a toga.

tribune An important officer in the Roman army.

typhoid A very serious disease that causes fever and diarrhoea. People often die from typhoid.

urn A large pot.

· INDEX ·

Page numbers in **bold** refer to illustrations.